FOREWORD - By Rick Sammon

Meet Joe Brady – awesome photo educator, excellent online and in-person communicator, wonderful photographer, passionate photo workshop leader, talented musician, serious fitness enthusiast and perhaps most important, loving husband and caring dad.

The aforementioned qualities make Joe a beloved member of the photo community and, I am proud to say, one of my good and most trusted friends.

Let's talk about trust. I trust you will enjoy learning about composition (and much more) from Joe on the pages of this book, into which Joe has poured his heart and soul. And as you go from page to page, you will trust Joe more and more as your virtual mentor, because he leaves no question unanswered and shares all he knows about the individual elements of making (and not just taking) a photograph.

If you have been on Joe's workshops, you know all this already, and know it to be true. If you have not had the pleasure of photographing side-by-side with Joe (which I have done many times), I encourage you to join one of his workshops. Again, I trust that you will learn a ton from this master of his craft.

I could go on and on about Joe and what I have learned from him, especially about color calibration and lighting. However, I don't want to keep you from diving into this book, which I suggest you refer to a few times and keep as a handy reference . . . because you may miss some important stuff the first time around. As Orson Wells said, "You need to watch a movie three times to appreciate all the messages, obvious and subtle." I feel the same idea applies to a book, especially this book, which is packed with so much practical information – not to mention beautiful photographs.

In closing, I will leave you with this thought: I hope you have the opportunity not only to photograph with Joe, but also to have the pleasure of having sushi with someone who I am proud to call my good and trusted friend.

Rick Sammon
www.ricksammon.com

"The world always seems brighter when you've just made something that wasn't there before".

Neil Gaiman

JOE BRADY

BETTER LANDSCAPES

The Power of Composition in Landscape Photography

Learn to Make *(don't just take!)* Better Photographs with Beauty and Impact

DEDICATION

This book is dedicated to my wife, Diane Bollen. You are my partner, my companion, my inspiration, my best friend and my True Love. Without you, this would never have happened.

To my children, Kyle and Elise, your love and affection makes my heart sing. Seeing you grow into such fine adults will always be my greatest achievement and joy.

THANKS

There are many people who have had impact on my photography, but my heartfelt thanks to two amazing photographers, Rick Sammon and Eddie Tapp. Your guidance and friendship mean the world to me.

ISBN: 978-0-578-25886-7 ©2021 Joe Brady.
All photography in this book ©2021 Joe Brady Photography

CONTENTS

"CUNNINGHAM CABIN VIEW" GRAND TETON NP

Why Should You Read this Book?

Because you want to make better Landscape Photos!

"DARK SKY MILKY WAY" GOBLIN VALLEY STATE PARK, GREEN RIVER, UT

WHAT'S IN THIS BOOK FOR YOU?

Let's start with a question: "Why do some landscape photos draw you in, while others only merit a quick glance?" I would like to help you learn to consistently create landscapes with impact and staying power - images that draw you in, that make you want to stay a while and explore.

Composition, light, color, visual cues and storytelling can all work hand-in-hand to make any photograph interesting and compelling. We are going to take a visual journey together and see how to recognize the elements that can greatly improve your Landscape Photography.

Ansel Adams once said,

"Landscape photography is the supreme test of the photographer - and often the supreme disappointment."

How can this be?

Both the problem and the opportunity of Landscapes is that there is so much to see. It's a problem because when there is so much beauty and so many interesting things, we want to have it all in each photo we take. This may record the scene, but it doesn't make for an interesting photograph.

One of our jobs as a photographer is to make it clear what we are asking the viewer to look at. Since they weren't there when you took the photo, they don't fully understand the entirety of the place, nor do they know where to look. If you haven't made the subject clear, or if there are too many details to look at, then the viewer will glance at the photo, say or think something like "that's nice" and then move on to something else.

In a successful Landscape Photograph, you are drawn into the scene, you should hear the sound of flowing water or crashing waves, experience the scents of the earth and sky, feel the warmth of the sun and the breeze on your skin. The viewer should enjoy the image and wish they were there. When this happens, your photograph has hit a home run.

I'd like to help you hit more home runs!

HOW TO READ THIS BOOK

The book is organized into a series of stories, but feel free to read the chapters in any order that interests you. If you take the time to closely examine the accompanying images along with the descriptive text, the thought process described in each section can help you better understand the elements that were considered to create the final image.

In addition to learning to see better composition, another important part of image creation is the processing of raw images and the shaping of color and light in Adobe Lightroom and Photoshop.

You can watch some in-depth step-by-step image edits for free on my Landscape Photography website:

www.joebradyphotography.com

Visit the tab named **"Landscape Composition and Editing"** for five videos, including three that are matched to chapters in this book.

Consider the flow of this book to be a conversation, not unlike one you might have if you were to accompany me on a Photography Workshop. The journey through the pages is meant to be educational, inspirational and enjoyable. Always remember that above all else, photography should be fun!

Let's get started!

"AFTERNOON AT SANKATY LIGHT" NANTUCKET, MA

WHY COMPOSITION?

I believe that composition is the most important aspect of Landscape Photography, and I couldn't find any books dedicated to this important subject. I recently heard from an author on a podcast, that he wrote a particular book "because he had to". When I found myself in bookstores and online looking for a book on this subject, I struck out, so ...

The book is organized into bite-sized sections that are discussions and explorations of what we can do to consistently create better Landscape images. I don't care what camera you use, and I don't care if your camera is your phone. That's not the point!

Great Landscape Photographs are about balance and composition, not about your gear. It's about seeing the whole, telling a story and capturing a moment forever.

So this book is about me sharing my love of photography with you, and explaining my approach and thought process when photographing the Landscape. Enjoy the journey and I hope you find inspiration to help create your own, powerful Landscape Photographs!

"TAGGART LAKE TRAIL" GRAND TETON NP

Realtors preach – 'Location, Location, Location,' while artists should preach – 'Composition, Composition, Composition.'

Doug Mays

CHAPTER ONE

Answer One Question and Start to Create Better Landscape Photos!

"ANTELOPE CANYON SPOTLIGHT"

PAGE, AZ

WHY AM I TAKING THIS PICTURE?

Whenever I'm at a location Photo Workshop, one question I suggest the photographers ask themselves is "Why am I taking this picture?" It seems like a simple request, but when you stop and really think about your answer, it can have big effects on the quality of your composition and the impact of all your photographs.

Understanding what made you stop in a particular spot to take a shot can go a long way towards improving the consistency and story telling of every image you take. Let's consider what happens when you ask yourself this question.

First, you slow down and begin to take a closer look everything that is in front of you. There are certainly elements that you missed at first, and they can be benefits or distractions in your composition.

Just taking in the environment and how it impacts your senses can give you a better feel of what to include in the frame.

As you scan the scene, you should decide on what you are asking the viewer to take from the photo. Is the subject clear? Is it large enough in the frame and are there other elements that compete for your attention? Even if you are making a photo just for yourself, are you capturing the feeling and story of the place so that you can revisit and enjoy it for years to come?

We want to encourage our viewers to not just look "at" the photo, but to slow down and look "into" the image as they explore and feel what it might have been like to be there.

Think of Landscape Photography as "A Portrait of the Place"

When you first arrive at a location, pay attention to what the light is doing. How does it shape your subject? Should you move to another spot? Should you wait a bit for a cloud to get into the right place, or for the sun to break through? When you have decided that "This is a great spot for my Landscape", are there small movements that could make it much better? You will be surprised at how much impact one step to the left or right can have on your composition.

Look around for foreground elements that can help lead you into the scene. When you have layers of foreground, middle distant and background, this creates dimension and invites the viewer to move deeper into the scene. Look for paths that lead to the subject. These can be actual physical paths made by foliage and/or rocks, bodies of still or moving water, or openings between trees.

Pay attention to the edges, pay attention to anything in the your viewfinder that draws you away from your intended subject. Look close at the percentage, height and size of all the spaces in the frame. When you think you have the perfect composition as you look through your camera, consider backing off on your zoom, or when using a prime lens, taking a few steps back. This will give you some room for cropping the image later on. Remember - you can always crop, but you can't "un-crop" if you didn't capture it in the first place.

If you put something of yourself into the image, that will always show.

"BELLVALE FARMS SUNSET" WARWICK, NY

PAY ATTENTION, BUT GO WITH YOUR GUT!

Composition is key for a successful Landscape Photograph, even if the light or weather doesn't cooperate. Since our cameras don't record tonal range and color the way our eyes see it, our raw images are going to need to be shaped in software to bring out the full beauty of the scene. We need to make adjustments of color and light to better tell the story of the place - and to make it clear why we stopped here to take this picture.

While you consider all of these options and elements, go with your gut! If it feels right to you, that's the picture you should take. Forget the "rules" and go with emotion. If you put something of yourself into the image, that will always show.

Now that we have started the conversation, let's head out into the field and explore the landscape together.

If it feels right to you, that's the picture you should take.

"PASSING STORM AT AGATHLA PEAK" KAYENTA, AZ

"Adopt the pace of nature. Her secret is patience."

Ralph Waldo Emerson

CHAPTER TWO

Move Left, Move Right, Squat Down, Follow a Path

Sometimes a step or two can present you with a much better photograph

COMPOSITION CHANGES WITH SMALL MOVEMENTS

Tree is too large in the frame

1

When you first arrive at a place it is a really good idea to walk around and take notice of all the possible elements to include in your photo. Pay attention to where the light is coming from, where the distractions are, and where you want to place the primary subject.

There is a tendency when you arrive at a place to just want to start shooting (yes, I do it too!), but your best photographs are going to happen when you slow down and get a feel for the place.

Let's take a closer look at a handful of shots from a walk around Nobska Light on Cape Cod and discuss the Pros and Cons of each image.

In Shot 1 at left, the lighthouse is sufficiently large in the frame, but the tree on the right is so big that it becomes a distraction that draws your eye away from the primary subject. When you have two objects in the frame that are of equal size and area, they visually compete with each other.

If you were to measure the physical height in the photo of both the lighthouse tower and the tree, they are pretty close to equal in size, and the tree is much wider. The size of the tree causes you to look away from the lighthouse to the right, and then nothing is stopping you from leaving the image.

Two of the key goals when composing our photos are to provide visual cues that guide the viewer to the subject, while also having elements that create a visual block that keeps from leaving the image. In this case the tree on the right does create a block, but it is too strong.

Could we crop this image and create a better composition? The image below is the same shot cropped on the right and up from the bottom. It's a start, but seems somewhat claustrophobic with no room to breath.

Let's move position and try again.

Better, but now too tight in the frame

SMALL STEPS, BIG IMPROVEMENTS!

Taking a few steps to the left and we have a much better composition in Shot 2! The large mass of foliage is gone and the branches in the middle left edge offer a nice fill into the bare, blue sky.

Since the foliage just to the right of the lighthouse building rises up slightly, it creates an slight obstacle to leaving the image. Rising slopes on the horizon caused by foliage, hills, etc. have the effect of rolling you back down that hill and guides the viewers eye back into the frame. This encourages them to linger a bit to explore more of the image, and that always a good thing.

One minor downside in the image above is that the lighthouse is pretty close to the middle of the frame. Since the tower is just slightly to the left of center, we can get away with it, but perhaps with a little bit of cropping we can improve the composition even more.

In Shot 3 we adjust the balance slightly, but with big effects. By cropping a little bit in from the left and taking off some from both the bottom and top of the image two things happen. The lighthouse is now a bit further left in the overall frame, and by cropping the image height, the tower is now larger in the photograph.

This gives our subject more visual strength and results in a pretty good composition. Moving the subject just a little bit more off center creates more visual motion in the photo. Even though the changes made were subtle, they have a big impact on the entire image. This one is a keeper!

LET'S WALK DOWN THE PATH A BIT ...

Entrance to the path is blocked

4

As we move down the hill, in Shot 4 we see a path that leads up to the lighthouse. This path is providing us with an actual physical way to get to the lighthouse, and that is a great start!

The problem however is that the path visually ends into the brush and doesn't give us a way to easily get there. This causes it to end up being a distraction that is disconnected from the rest of the scene.

In addition, since the path is light in color surrounded by the dark green foliage, our eyes are drawn to it. Once again, since it is on the right side of the frame, this has a tendency to lead us out of the image and looking for something else to catch our interest. That said, this isn't a terrible image, but we can do better.

A little further down the hill and slightly to the left, we now start to see the how the path leads us to the lighthouse. Physical paths are great elements to guide the viewer both into the scene and to the subject. So what's the downside?

Since we are further from the lighthouse, the area from the bottom of the frame to the base of the lighthouse is as tall or maybe even slightly taller than the height of the lighthouse.

This size allows the foliage in the base to compete for our attention and takes away focus on the lighthouse. The large base of green foliage, which serves as a nice base pedestal for our subject, now takes up almost half of the image. In addition, with the horizon line ending almost halfway up in the image, it splits the photo into two halves and this weakens the composition.

Perhaps if we take a few steps to the left the problem will be fixed.

Too Much Sky!

Too Much Foreground!

6

7

Taking a few steps to the left and perhaps one or two steps down the hill and we have a better composition in Shot 6. The path to the lighthouse is clear and the foliage rising on the right side of the image creates a gentle visual block that rolls the eyes back to the subject.

We have the makings here of a nice composition, but one important edit remains - cropping! When there are parts of your photo that don't contain anything that contributes to the scene, crop it out. Shot 6 above has a lot of cloudless, blue sky above the lighthouse that doesn't contribute. On the bottom, there might be a bit too much path so that it competes slightly with the lighthouse tower, so let's crop a bit here as well.

The final crop is an extremely important step towards finalizing your image. By eliminating what doesn't contribute, the composition becomes stronger, because the primary subject then fills a larger percentage of the frame. This gives the subject more 'weight" in the photo and draws the viewer's eyes.

The image that we then have in Shot 7 above contains all of the elements for a great composition. The path in the lower right guides you into the scene, while the foliage on the right edge keeps you in the photo as it slopes upwards. Having more environment in the composition helps tell more of a story about where the lighthouse "lives".

"NOBSKA LIGHT" WOODS HOLE, CAPE COD, MA

By cropping out the blank space, the lighthouse fills a larger percentage of the frame and is the most dominant element. Between Shot 3 and Shot 7, we have two great views of Nobska Light that would both make fine prints.

"Look deep into nature, and then you will understand everything better."

Albert Einstein

CHAPTER THREE

Let's Take a Hike Together

Discussing what you see can stir up creative thinking

FINDING A GREAT PHOTOGRAPH

"DESERT REFLECTIONS" ARCHES NATIONAL PARK, MOAB, UT

During a recent Photo Workshop visit to Arches National Park, we were gifted with a rare, evening rain. I consider this as a gift because Arches after a rainfall takes on a completely different color palette.

The red sandstone typically has a uniformity of color shade when it is dry, but add some rainfall, and it looks like you just increased the contrast of all your photographs.

"COURTHOUSE TOWERS" ARCHES NATIONAL PARK, MOAB, UT

The overnight rain provided a rare treat the following day. Join me on the hike we took that morning in Arches National Park.

Our first destination was a hike around the back of a formation named Courthouse Towers. This is always a beautiful place, but after a rain, the magic happens. There are deposits of hard rock around the surface behind the towers, and they hold on to some of the rain, creating shallow puddles of rainwater that create the most amazing reflections. This is what we were after for our photography that morning, and you can view a results on the preceeding page with "Reflections Behind Courthouse Towers".

After we came around the towers and back to the main road, we found ourselves just a bit south of our next destination, an iconic formation named "The Three Gossips".

At first there weren't many clouds behind the formation, but stopping to watch the sky, we could see that clouds were moving our way. It looked like it was going to make for some nice photographs.

As we walked along the road towards the Three Gossips, I took a series of photos to capture how the light was constantly changing. Some of the shots are nothing special to look at, but others had some potential. Let's start our hike and we'll discuss the images.

Shown below, our initial view of the Gossips may be interesting, but there is a large rock formation right in front of our primary subject. This obviously overpowers the scene and is quite the distraction. Let's move a bit closer and see if the view and composition improve.

Big rock in the way!

Now this is a getting a lot more interesting and may deserve a closer edit. The brush, bushes and twisted tree in the foreground provide a window to the Gossips and a nice frame to look through. Some cropping off the top and perhaps some darkening of the soil at bottom and we might have a keeper!

As a cloud passes in front of the sun, it casts a shadow on the formation. This combined with the darker than usual tone of the Gossips because of the overnight rain gives them an interesting look. The blurry tree however is a distraction, but has some potential. Let's move back and try this again.

Backing up and going wider on the lens created this interesting framing. The trees and foreground however are a bit too overpowering in the scene. Let's crop the image.

The new crop below simplfies the scene and this works much better. The foreground tree is an interesting element and could be considered the main subject as it frames the Three Gossips. The rock formations in the background draw your eye as you enter the frame, and the bush at the lower right adds a visual block to keep you in the photo.

Needs a bit of cropping above - looks much better below!

We keep walking closer, but the clouds haven't arrived into the scene yet. We can see them approaching from the right, so let's wait a bit.

Some light clouds have moved in and one has positioned itself right above the heads of the Gossips. There is too much foreground, but that could easily be cropped off. Perhaps with some light painting and the appropriate crop, this one might just work.

Another cloud passes in front of the sun causing a line of dark shadow that forms a leading line right to the Gossips. Cropping both bottom and top turns this into a more panoramic feel and eliminates the unnecessary parts of the image - a little bit more light painting with some darkening at the lower left corner and it's a keeper!

Big Distraction!

1

Still a
Distraction!

2

As we get closer, in Image 1 on the left, we now have shadows cast by Courthouse Towers which at this point on our hike is right across the road behind us. This dark foreground creates a really nice base for the image. The problem here is that the Boulder on the left is too big and dominates the frame. This is something you have to be attentive to when you look through the viewfinder - avoid distractions to the main subject.

In Image 2 below, moving a bit to the right makes the boulder smaller, but the image still doesn't quite work. The best solution would have been to take a few steps to the right and then squat down a bit lower.

How about a vertical composition? The layers of light from bottom dark to light mid-distance to deep blue sky create a lot of visual movement. Placing the Gossips slightly to the right adds more movement as well. This image would work well as a framed print placed on a section of vertical wall in your home, particularly if printed large enough. The vertical is a successful composition because it includes all of the important elements and eliminates anything not necessary to tell the story of the place.

Since we generally view a vertical image from the bottom up, the shadow foreground forms a nice visual base upon which the rest of the image sits. The mid-ground has several layers of rock, brush and then fallen stone before we get to the pristine formation of the Three Gossips.

Here we see the entire valley open up to the Three Gossips and we get a clearer picture of the place where this formation lives. This image could work well as a print, but it would have to be large to really work - probably 30" or wider. The reason for this size requirement is that the primary formation takes up too little room in the composition. The green bush at the bottom right is as big as the formation and competes with it. One solution would be to crop up and cut off the bottom third of the bush.

Another option would be to make this a vertical. One of the great things about shooting your images horizontal is that you can always crop the shot to a vertical - can't do that with a vertical Raw file!

As we look at the vertical composition at right, there are both physical paths and barriers that help the viewer navigate the image. At the bottom center (1) we have a winding, physical path that presents us with a way to walk our eyes to the Gossips. The bush on the lower right (2) and the edge of the boulder (3) block us from leaving the image and guide us along as well. If you were going to walk closer, this is your path.

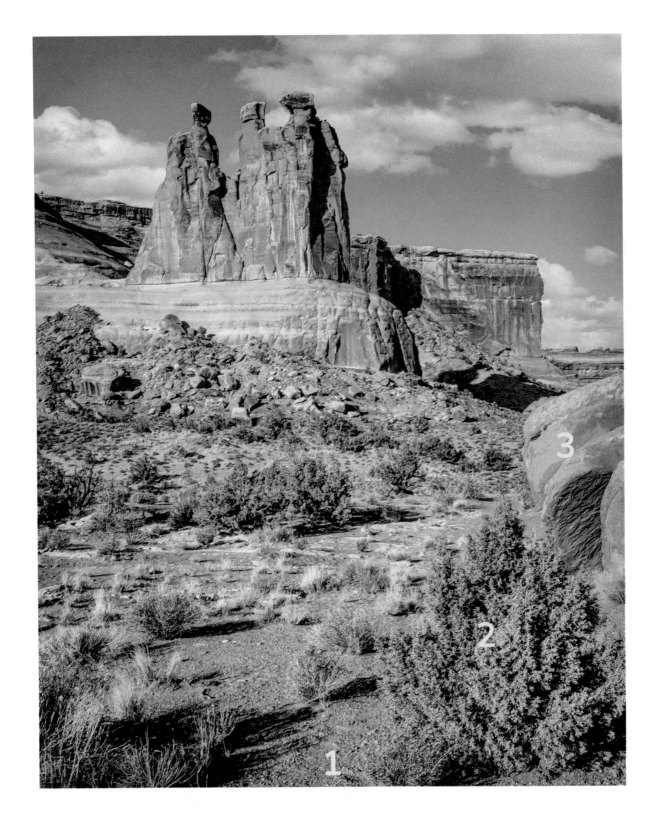

The vertical composition works nicely, but I do like having a sense of the entire valley and the environment where the Three Gossips live. Let's go back to the original shot and try a horizontal, panoramic crop.

Here we see two versions of the panoramic crop. They are very similar, but subtly and powerfully different. The smaller image on the top has the Three Gossips slightly left of center and the boulders are still there to block you from leaving the image - BUT - the space to the right of the boulders and the downward slope of the distant formation present a way out of the image.

Since the boulders are a strong element, your eyes are drawn to them and then off you go leaving the image. This problem could be improved by cropping off a bit of the right edge, but let's see what happens when we also add some to the left edge.

The image at bottom seems to break the rule of not putting your subject dead-center in an image, but in this case, it's the right choice to make. Everything in the images leads to the primary formation. The Three Gossips is also the only thing that pierces the sky, and this adds visual power as well.

The downward slope with shadow on the upper left leads you down the mesa right to the Gossips, and the small butte right at the edge keeps you from leaving.

When you get there, your eyes bounce you back to the middle because the rock formation blocks the way out. Lastly, there is also a bit of path remaining at bottom center to walk you in. By cropping off the bottom and a bit off the right, everything in this photograph now works!

These fine changes in cropping have a powerful effect on how the eye travels through a photograph. If you want the viewer to really look into your photo, paying attention to these details can go a long way toward making that happen.

"The earth has music for those who listen."
William Shakespeare

CHAPTER FOUR

Look at the Details When Composing Your Shot

It's the little things that support the Main Attraction

Sometimes a Landscape that initially says "Horizontal", actually works better when shot vertically. It forces you to simplify and concentrate on the main subject

Image 1

SEEING COMPOSITION DIFFERENCES IN THE FIELD

When you slow and take time to examine the scene you are about to photograph, looking for fine differences can have a big impact on your final image. Of course, there is nothing wrong with taking multiple shots from slightly different positions, and changing the height and zoom on your lens, but also consider that if you like to take a lot of photos, there will be many more to sort through.

Let's take a look at another series of shots captured in Arches National Park. These images were taken just off the main park road at the northern end of what is called the Park Avenue Trail.

The light this morning was absolutely spectacular and the clouds were stunning as well. I decided to capture a handful of shot both horizontally and vertically to create a different feel and focus for the place. While I originally thought of this as a "Landscape" oriented place, I found that the verticals or "Portrait mode" shots were also beautiful, and in some ways had even more impact. Let's look closer.

At first glance, the three shots look very similar, and each would make a nice print. When you slow down and look closer, they are actually quite different and that is the purpose of this exercise.

As I captured these shots, the clouds were moving quickly across the sky, so each shot has different light patterns falling on the primary structure. While I do like the light better in one of the three shots, it's the composition differences that have the biggest impact.

Starting with Image 1 on the left page, the light is nice, but the primary subject is a bit too close to dead center of the frame. If I had backed off a bit on the zoom, I might have had a bit more room for positioning - my bad! There is a nice, clear path at the bottom of the image that leads you right to the main formation, but once again, it too is almost dead center.

When you create a photograph in Portrait mode, you are making the viewer read the image from bottom to top, and while that is just fine, when the paths and the subject are in the center of the frame, your eyes have a tendency to make that straight line right to the subject.

This direct line to the subject keeps the viewer from stopping along the way and taking in the other elements in the photo. The eyes go straight to the subject and then may simply leave the photograph to look at something else. Now this shot isn't terrible, but the next two are better.

In the second shot (Image 2), the light is possibly the most beautiful and the path on the left side creates a more twisted route to the subject. This forces the eye to consider the other objects along the path. You pause to take in the foreground elements as you walk your eyes to the peak. By having just a little bit more on the left side of the frame, the position of our subject gets pushed just a little more to the right, and this change in balance adds more motion to the photograph.

My only minor complaint for this image is that the brush at the bottom center of the frame could have used a bit more space under it. By not having any of the sandy path, you temporarily get stuck there. I could have probably fixed this by squatting down a bit and including a little more of the closer foreground.

The third shot (Image 3) fixes the foreground problem and the zoom is backed off a bit more which allows the main formation to be a little further to the right. This works nicely, but now the main subject is smaller than in Image 2. After spending some time staring at Image 3, I realized I had two possible choices. I could simply crop the top of the image which would decrease the amount of sky and make the primary peak larger in the frame. *OR* - I could take both Image 2 and Image 3 and composite them together with Adobe Photoshop.

Not quite enough room
under the brush

Great Light on
Primary Formation

Image 2

Primary Formation getting a bit small

Nice having a bit more room at the lower left and bottom of the image

Image 3

49

RESULT OF THE PHOTOSHOP COMPOSITE

The Original - Image 1

I knew this would be a somewhat complex edit, but the final result on the right was so worth it! I was able to keep the beautiful light on the Peak, *AND* include the greater room provided to the path, *and* a little more more space on the left side of the image.

When you compare the original (Image 1) with the final composite shot on the facing page, you can clearly see how much better the light is, and how the composition has more balance and flow.

"MORNING ON THE PARK AVENUE TRAIL"
ARCHES NATIONAL PARK, MOAB, UT

Here's the final composite of images 2 and 3. The foreground of image 3 was better, but the position, size and light of the primary subject in Image 2 was more dramatic.

Final Composite Image

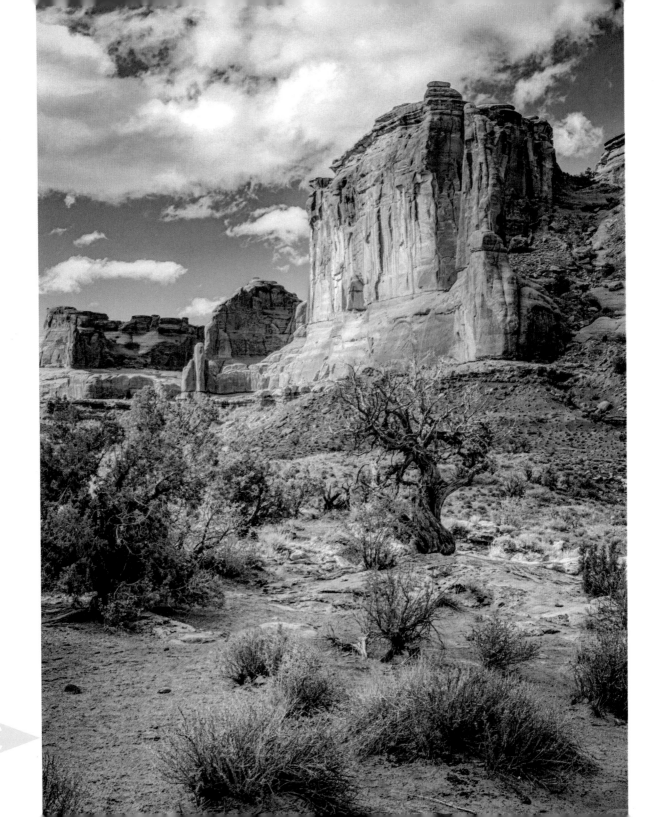

LET'S LOOK AT THIS IN LANDSCAPE MODE

While we're here, let's take a look at the horizontal, "Landscape mode" shot of the same location. I captured a selection if images here as well, but I didn't realize until after I downloaded my images that night that there was a bush almost dead center of the frame that stopped you from entering the scene.

I had to find the image with this distraction as far to one side as possible while still making the entire shot work. I still needed some more room to get both the bush and the open space between the two distant formations out of the center of the image - otherwise I would be dealing with a photo that looked like a pair of rocky goalposts waiting for a ball to be kicked through.

Goalposts!

Bad Bush!

I brought the best shot into Photoshop for some adjustments. By selecting the entire right half of the image and extending the canvas to the right, I used Content Aware Scale to stretch *(rather than compress)* the image to the right a bit. This added just the right amount of image on the right side to make the composition work.

The result is below and I feel that the balance of the composition has much more motion that an image with the primary features dead-center.

Though I like this photograph a lot, for it to really work, it would need to be a large print - 36" wide or more. There is a lot to look at and a big print would do the best job of telling the story of the place.

While I really like the image below, I still prefer the vertical composite on the previous page. The simplicity of subject, beautiful light and the harmony of the elements simply has more impact.

"When people ask me what equipment I use
– I tell them my eyes."

Anonymous

CHAPTER FIVE

Some Useful Tech Stuff, Explained Simply

What's the Best Camera for Me, and what are those graph things the camera keeps showing me?

WHICH CAMERA SHOULD I USE?

I ASK YOU "WHICH CAMERA DO YOU HAVE?"

Thisisacommonquestionforphotographers and since we all have a tendency to be gear-heads, we are always excited to see the newest, next best thing. Are there specific capabilities to look for when choosing a camera? That question depends on what type of photography you wish to pursue. For general photography, you can get wonderful results with pretty much any camera on the market, and in some cases by just using your phone. To confirm this claim, I'm putting a couple of hidden iPhone shots in this book!

When you have more specific needs, there are lots of question to ask that will influence your camera system decision. For those into specific photo specialties like capturing birds in flight, action sports, and astrophotography, there is special gear and lens considerations that will improve that experience. However, there is one limiting factor that always needs to be addressed first ...

DO YOU UNDERSTAND HOW YOUR CAMERA?

This doesn't mean that you need to know every camera setting, option and menu item to be successful with your photography. Today's cameras have a ridiculous amount of options in their menus, the vast majority of which you will never need to know about. But what you do need to know is having enough knowledge about how things work to keep the camera out of the way. You don't want your lack of comfort with the camera to keep you from getting the photo.

Your camera is a tool you need to become familiar with. You need to know enough so that when great photos presents themselves, the camera buttons and settings won't stop you from successfully getting the shot you are after.

ARE THERE CAMERAS THAT DO A BETTER JOB AT LANDSCAPE PHOTOGRAPHY?

It used to be that the larger the sensor your camera had, the better tonal range performance you would get. Since many landscapes challenge the dynamic range of even the best cameras available, having more dynamic range is certainly a plus. Today's APS-C and even Micro Four-Thirds sensors have a lot of tonal range that can be sufficient for most any situation. Over the past few years, I have used camera systems from every major manufacturer and found them all capable of capturing great images.

What much more important is to have a camera that you are comfortable with. It feels nice in your hands, the controls are easy to get to and the entire layout of the body and lens makes sense to you.

When you have a comfortable camera and spend some time getting to know how it operates, you will reach for it knowing that you are going to get a nice photo!

THE SINGLE MOST IMPORTANT BIT OF GEAR

I have seen people spend many thousands of dollars on the biggest, latest and greatest camera gear who are incapable of creating a great photograph, while I have seen others with the most basic camera or just their phone create stunning results. This is of course because the most important bit of gear is you.

You are the one making the decisions about where to point the camera, what to include, where to move, and when to press the shutter. Provided you have the best exposure possible, the key to successful Landscape Photography is composition and storytelling.

Learn enough about your camera system so that it doesn't keep you from creating the image you want. This provides you with the freedom to put something of yourself into every photo you take - and that's the most important part of great photography.

WHAT IS THIS HISTOGRAM THING?

and what is it trying to tell me?

THE HISTOGRAM ISN'T ALL THAT MYSTERIOUS, BUT IT TRIES TO BE!

I know a lot of people are confused about the histogram, but it really is fairly simple and more importantly, it provides all the information you need to get the best exposure possible. The confusion happens because it usually provides you with a lot of info you don't really need.

SO WHAT EXACTLY IS IT SHOWING ME?

The Histogram is simply a graph showing the relative brightness of all the individual pixels in your image. The left wall of the graph represents pure black, and the right wall represents pure white. In most cases you want to avoid having your graph hit either wall, but sometimes it can't be helped.

Where the confusion comes from is the mountain-looking shape in the middle! Well here's the easy answer - in most cases it isn't important at all! What the "mountain" shape of the graph is showing you is the amount of pixels with each brightness value in your image. Who cares?

If you take a picture of a snowman in a snowy field on a bright, sunny day with blue skies, then the "mountain" in the graph will be all pushed to the right - at least when it is exposed correctly. That's because there are very few dark pixels in the image, with the exception of the coal you used for the eyes.

Conversely, if you take a picture of a black cat on a freshly coated driveway, when your picture is exposed correctly, the "mountain" part of the graph will be pushed to the left edge. That's simply because almost all of the pixels in the image are dark. Now go clean the cat's paws before it walks around the house.

Most landscape images will challenge your camera's abilities to capture light to dark because there is so much tonal range in outdoor scenes. You have both bright skies and puffy, white clouds and then dark shadows in the shade and under rocks. In digital photography, it is most important to protect any highlights where the detail is important. This means you don't have to worry about specular highlights (like the sun reflecting off of a chromed bumper) or bright lights shining at you, but you do need to protect the details in clouds, snow and bright sand. If you overexpose these highlights, all detail is gone forever.

When you protect the highlights, it is common for the image on the back of your camera to look way too dark. That is something very easy to fix when you process photos later on. To get this most perfect exposure, trust the histogram. Check the image on your camera and bring up the histogram. This is typically done as you cycle through the Info button choice with the image displayed.

Trust the Histogram to Show You Everything You Need for a Perfect Exposure!

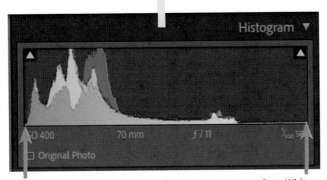

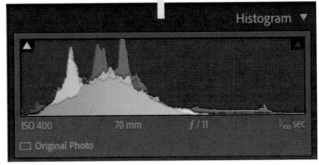

Pure Black

Pure White

Let's take a look at the two images above and their histograms as shown in Lightroom. By the way, don't let the colors confuse you - in fact, ignore them!

The left image is the raw file. It looks really dark, but you could argue that the exposure is near perfect. When you look at the histogram base from left to right, you can see that it goes right up to the black edge on the left, and right up to the white edge on the right. The majority of the "mountain" in the graph is to the left, or shadow side, but this shouldn't be a surprise.

It is easy to see that most of the image is pretty dark. This exposure was captured to try to keep the setting sun from blowing out too much of the surrounding middle of the frame.

The image on the right is the same file after adjusting the shadows and exposure in Lightroom. The histogram still goes from the left to right edge, but the "mountain" has been shifted towards the middle. It is still towards the left or dark side of the histogram, but again, the image is mostly darker.

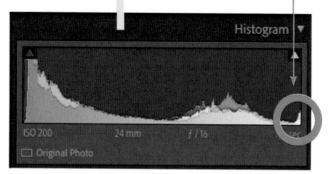

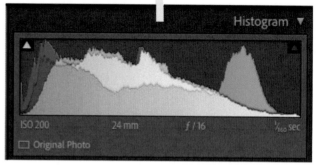

Above are another pair of before-after edits and what happens to the histogram. The image on the left is the raw file. You can see the graph covering from left to right, but this time there is a bit stuck on the right side wall. This means that there is some pure white in the image. You can darken pure white in lightroom, but you won't be able to get back any detail. In this case, the upper right corner of the image is the sun behind some clouds, so there wasn't any detail there to worry about.

In the right side image, we see the final edit of the photo and now our "mountain" graph extends all across the histogram. This shows us there are lots of pixels in the image that go from dark to bright.

This matches what we see with our eyes, so this is great! Ignore the height of the graph peaks - they are not important.

As long as the "mountain" is not hitting the right edge of the graph, you are safe! If you have the sun in the frame, then expect part of the graph stuck to the right wall. If the graph doesn't go anywhere near the right edge and there are very bright elements in the scene (like white clouds, snow or sunny sand), that means you have underexposed the shot and might want to consider taking another one with a little more light let in.

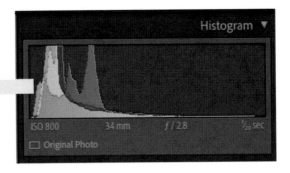

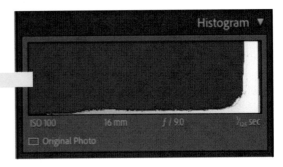

These last two samples show what a correct histogram may look like when the scene is mostly dark or mostly light. The top image of the boats pre-sunrise is very dark, but if you take notice of the histogram, you see that while it is pushed to the left, it never actually makes it to the edge. That means no pure black and we can adjust the shadows if desired.

The image below of the snowy barn is mostly a scene of almost pure white, but if you look closely at the histogram, the graph never hits the right edge. That means that the snow still has some detail in it. This is what a snowy histogram should look like!

TURNING ON "THE BLINKIES"

If you are new to this histogram thing, digital cameras have the ability to show you "highlight warnings". These tell you that parts of the image are in danger of being overexposed. You can then adjust the exposure until these flashing white warnings (know as the "blinkies") go away.

Once you become comfortable with reading the histogram, I recommend turning off the "blinkies". They are very conservative in protecting overexposure and are costing you up to 10% of your camera's tonal range. Learn to read the histogram, and you can be sure of the best exposure, every time!

"The eye should learn to listen before it looks."

Robert Frank

CHAPTER SIX

My, What a Big Zoom Lens You Have!

From near to far, your lens choice changes
what is important in the picture

THE EFFECT OF FOCAL LENGTH ON YOUR PHOTOS

JOHN MOULTON BARN, GRAND TETON NATIONAL PARK
27MM FROM 10 YARDS AWAY, 10:35AM, 10/9/20

The combination of your distance to the subject and the choice of lens focal length or "zoom" on your lens has an enourmous effect on the feeling of your photos. The images on these pages are of the same barn in Grand Teton, but shot at 27mm and 135mm full frame equivalent focal length lenses.

In the shot just above, by standing close to the barn, the building and surrounding fence are large while the mountain range in the distance is small.

Now take a look to the image on the right. When we walk back 100 yards or so and go to a 135mm zoom, the peak of Grand Teton soars above the barn!

The mood and focus of each image is very different because of our distance to the subject and the choice of lens focal length. It's hard to believe that these are shots of the same place! Focal Length, standing position and time of day all have big effects on the mood and focus of a landscape.

JOHN MOULTON BARN
GRAND TETON NATIONAL PARK

THIS PAGE:
135MM FROM 100 YARDS
AWAY,
9:23AM, 10/7/17

The two shots on these facing pages were taken one day apart, but at different times of day and with different focal lengths.

The image above was taken late in the day, 6:10PM on October 2, 2020 with the lens set at 36mm. Because of its north-south orientation, the Grand Tetons are not usually great subjects near sunset, but with the combination of the backlit barn, the smoky haze on the mountains, and the warm colors of the fall foliage, it has a lovely mood.

Because of the time of day, lens settings and position and distance from the barn, the background shares the stage with the changing colors of the leaves and the sky reflection in the stream.

The foreground elements including the fallen leaves, grass and stream start you into the scene, and the branches frame the barn and peaks, while also keeping you from leaving the image too soon.

This photo of the same barn was taken the next day at 10:30AM with the lens set at 50mm. By taking a few steps to the right, I wanted to see if using the trees on either side to frame the scene would work. I chose this spot because there wasn't a cloud in the sky and I wanted to have some interest around the barn and peaks.

Notice how much taller the Peak of Grand Teton gets with the change in focal length! I needed both the barn and mountain to have more impact so that they could successfully compete with the surrounding trees and the 50mm focal length made that happen.

T.A. MOULTON BARN GRAND TETON NATIONAL PARK

OPPOSITE PAGE: 36MM AT 6:10PM, 10/2/20

THIS PAGE: 50MM AT 10:30AM, 10/3/20

If you have never been to Grand Teton National Park, these famous barns, located on a dirt road named Mormon Row, provide so many photo opportunities all day long. There are two similarly constructed barns named after their first residents. The John Moulton barn above and the T.A. Moulton Barn on the bottom at right. I would guess that the scene above is probably the most photographed spot in the park.

Since the mountains run north-south, sunrise is by far the most popular time and lots of photographers get there early to claim their spots. Fortunately, most people pay attention to not getting in the way of other photographer's shots, though occassionally, decorum breaks down.

These photos were taken years apart, and this shows that returning to the same place is certainly not a waste of time. The different times of day, different standing positions and different focal lengths all create very different views and feelings of this place.

Just because an iconic view is photographed by many others, doesn't mean that you can't create an image that is both unique and beautiful!

JOHN & T.A. MOULTON BARNS

ABOVE: 70MM AT 9:56AM, 10/10/17

OPPOSITE TOP: 44MM AT 4:16PM, 9/26/14

OPPOSITE BOTTOM: 24MM AT 6:07PM, 10/2/12

"Your first 10,000 photographs are your worst."

Henri Cartier-Bresson

CHAPTER SEVEN

Ooooh, Let's Go Back Again!

You missed a lot last time you were there

"MORNING AT MESA ARCH"
CANYONLANDS NATIONAL PARK, MOAB, UT

When you come across a strong, dynamic scene with an obvious, even iconic view and subject, chances are that there will be many different points of view that work for the photo.

One such place is Mesa Arch in Canyonlands National Park. I have photographed this beautiful spot many times over the past years and regardless of the weather, sun and clouds, I am always able to get some wonderful variations that gift me with new interpretations of this familiar place. The image at left is one of my personal favorites, so let's discuss why.

Sometimes it is possible for the subject to be the entire scene. For this to work, I feel there need to be secondary subjects and sightlines to follow into and around the image. Obviously Mesa Arch is the star here, but the reflecting light turning the bottom of the arch bright orange (1) is something that totally grabs your eye.

The bright canyon and formations under the arch in the distance also draw the eye and you can't help looking through the opening and gazing at the distant features (2). One small feature in this shot is a formation named "The Washerwoman" (3), though it is too small here. Were this a big print - 36" or larger across - that feature would be more visible with the details easier to see.

The big and little shrubs at bottom left and on top of the arch (4) create a counterpoint that frame the scene, and their dark shades, contrast in color and organic shapes draw your eye, which once again leads you to the light under the arch. The base stone under the arch (5) provides just enough pedestal for the entire scene to rest.

There is nothing in this image that does not in some way contribute to the scene, and while there are many different interpretations possible, this beautiful image certainly works. I captured this shot in 2015 and never get tired of looking at it. Any image that stands the test of time is certainly a successful composition!

One shot that everyone who visits Mesa Arch wants to capture is the sun starburst just under the arch. By shooting at a small aperture like f18 or f22, the starburst appears.

I personally prefer the sun just at or over the top of the arch, but my favorite shots don't show the sun at all. Why is that?

The sun starburst is a very strong graphic element and can easily overpower everything else in the scene. I find the arch so beautiful along with the canyon in the distance, that I prefer the focus to be there.

In the three panoramas on the right, the focus of each image changes based on what is included in the frame. In the top image (1), the sunburst is the strongest point, then your eyes go to the orange underside and the canyon beyond.

In the middle shot (2), by cropping off the top of the arch, this photo is all about the distant canyon as the arch itself becomes a frame for the image.

Lastly, the bottom shot (3) shows the entire arch and how is fits into the rest of the landscape. While probably the least "artistic" shot, it does the best job of showing where Mesa Arch "lives".

By the way, if you were ever curious about what Mesa Arch looks like at sunrise, below are some examples of all the photographers lined up. Come an hour later, and it's all yours!

You initially wouldn't think that a vertical shot like the one above could work here. I really like this shot with its small section of arch. It showcases the small shrub on the top and the Washerwoman formation under the arch.

By simplifying the composition this way, the image is more intimate. There is less to look at, but the remaining elements are interesting and their shapes still draw your eyes. When there are fewer things in the frame, they work in a small print.

1

2

3

"Every portrait that is painted with feeling is a portrait of the artist, not of the sitter."

Oscar Wilde

CHAPTER EIGHT

Be Still and See the Future, Grasshopper*

What comes next just might be exactly what you were waiting for

* You are at least as old as me if you understand this reference from the "King Fu" TV Series during the early 1970's

HAVE PATIENCE AND BE CAREFUL WITH CROPPING

"FIRST LIGHT", CAPE MAY, NJ

Landscape Photography sometime presents you with a beautiful scene as soon as you arrive on location. In fact, sometimes you are jumping out of the car to capture the beautiful light before it changes or the clouds move into a less desirable position.

Other times it requires a lot of patience. Taking the time to watch the atmospheric conditions and light can pay off when you are willing to wait. This is one of the reasons that trying to do Landscape Photography on some sort of organized bus trip is a true exercise in frustration for a photographer. Being told that you have 30 minutes at the The Grand Canyon has to be one of the worst things to ever hear!

This series of images was captured in Cape May, NJ early one morning. This took place during a photography conference and I had brought a handful of friends to one of my favorite photography spots. We arrived about an hour before sunrise with plans to photograph the commercial fishing fleet getting ready to head out for the day.

It was pretty dark when we first arrived, but as we approached sunrise, the horizon began to glow a deep magenta-red. The boats and their lights created beautiful reflections in the water and the brightening sky was creating a great scene to photograph.

SOMETHING WAS
ABOUT TO DISTURB
THE CALM!

SO WHAT HAPPENED NEXT?

This sequence of images tells the story of the morning. As we stood on a dock watching the light, all was quiet and still. It was very peaceful and decorative, but without much of a story - yet.

As our group was shooting this scene *(Shot 1)*, we heard the motor of a small boat coming our way. It was a little skiff with a lone fisherman heading out. Immediately, our group started to complain that this little boat was going to cause a big wake and lots of ripples in the water.

Since they all thought it was going to ruin the shot, all of them (it was 5 or 6 people) decided to leave the dock and look around for some other shots.

I told them I was just going to wait on the dock and would see them again in a bit. I didn't bother explaining my reasoning, but I saw something that they apparently missed. To the right side of the fishing fleet was a bit of open water. As the little skiff got closer, I could visualize him becoming a wonderful counterpoint in the otherwise empty space as he motored past the waiting fleet. That photo is the full page shot at the beginning of this chapter.

The fisherman in his small skiff did not disappoint, *(Shot 2)* and I was able to capture an image that remains one of my favorites to this day. The lesson in this story is to have patience and spend some time visualizing what you would ideally like the photograph to look like.

4

By the way, my colleagues were not completely wrong about the ripples on the water disturbing the calm of the scene. The image at bottom left *(Shot 3)* shows the skiff heading out into the bay and the ripples do ruin the mood.

After the skiff turned the corner, the remaining ripples created a very painterly set of reflections for the boats and their lights *(Shot 4)*. Certainly not my favorite image here, but still interesting. However, something is wrong with this image.

By cropping the space around the boats, they do become larger in the frame but that feels uncomfortable. The image is now cramped. Everything is so close to the edges of the frame and the entire photograph has no room to breath. This claustrophobic feeling often happens when you crop too much - and yes, it is possible to do this!

Having subject matter fit every inch of the composition is uncomfortable and you lose the lines of shape and light that lead you into the picture.

"THAT SMALL BOAT IS GOING TO RUIN THE REFLECTIONS! I'M GOING SOMEWHERE ELSE!"

The image above *(Shot 5)* improves the tight crop shown in Shot 4. Including more water gives the scene a bit of room to breath and a more peaceful feeling. The water is stronger than the boats with a simple adjustment to how the photograph is cropped.

On the page opposite, compare Shot 2 to the *"First Light"* image *(shown bottom right and also much larger on the first page of this section)* and notice how the space around, above and below the boats in *"First Light"* tells a better story of the place.

Because of the tighter crop in Shot 2, the small skiff is taking up more of the frame. To best tell the story, the skiff needs to appear small to create the contrast in sizes. Also take notice of the how wake behind the small boat is cut short in Shot 2. This weakens the timeline of the story about where the fisherman came from and how he entered the scene.

Make it a habit to capture more of the scene than you feel you need, because you can always crop later, but you can't get it back if you didn't capture it.

Cropping is a fine-tuning best saved for when you process your photos.

Remember it's best to capture more than you think you need!

Wake from boat is too small, overall crop is too tight!

"First Light"

"Great things are not done by impulse, but a series of small things brought together."

Vincent Van Gogh

CHAPTER NINE

There are no Rules, but some Guidelines Might Help

Make your photos stronger with careful placement of the subject

THE "RULE OF THIRDS" - FRIEND OR FOE?

Most photographers are aware of the concept known as "The Rule of Thirds". In its basic form this is a recommendation that you put your subject 1/3rd of the way from one side and top and bottom of the frame. Imagine you divide your viewfinder with evenly spaced lines left and right, top and bottom to form a 3x3 grid, with 9 evenly sized spaces. In fact many cameras have the ability to overlay such a grid in your viewfinder.

If you look at the sample image above of the Rule of Thirds grid, the philosophy is to place your subject on or near one of the intersections around the central rectangle.

In theory, if you follow this "Rule", it will keep you from placing your subjects too near the center or near the edge of the frame.

This is not a terrible thing! Rather than a rule, it is a basic guideline that can help get you started with image composition. Unfortunately, placing your subjects to these points can begin to feel both forced and static. You could find that all of your subjects end up in the same place.

Might there be a better option?

Make Friends with The Golden Ratio!

When you are ready to really improve the composition of your images, there is another guideline that I feel creates much better, and much more natural feeling results - it's called "The Golden Ratio". Without getting into Fibonacci Sequences and Classical Architecture, the Golden Ratio works on a ratio of 1.6 to 1 rather than equal thirds. It occurs naturally in nature and for some reason, it resonates with the human mind.

The Golden Ratio may take a little more time to feel obvious to you, but with a little but of practice, you will wonder why you didn't always use this guide.

Take a look at the samples on the following pages, and notice how many of them naturally follow the Golden Ratio. By the way, there's also a variation on this called the Golden Spiral where you can place important elements all along the spiral. This works really well for certain types of images.

Here's the best news! All three of these guides (and several more) can be accessed when you bring up the Crop Tool in both Lightroom and Photoshop. Simply choose the options under Tools, select the Crop Guide Overlay and give it a try.

While there are certainly times when the Rule of Thirds works just fine, take a look at these images with the Rule of Thirds grid on the left, and the Golden Ratio grid on the right image. In these samples, the primary subject naturally falls on the Golden Ratio grid. If the Rule of Thirds were used here, the primary subject here would be pushed more to the right.

This is of course a bit subjective, but I find the balance in most all of my photography works much better when I stay relatively close to the Golden Ratio.

In the shot above at Kanarra Falls (Kanarraville, UT), the water flowing down the slot canyon is just off-center enough without adding to the mass of rock on the left.

By the way, I have people ask about the strange log on the right of the falls. It's actually a set of ladder steps for those who wish to continue hiking up the falls. If you keep going, there is another waterfall further on, right at the end of the slot canyon as it opens to the sky.

This panoramic shot taken at Ruby Beach (Olympic National Park) doesn't do well following the Rule of Thirds. If we stuck to that grid it would have caused the primary subject - in this case a Sea-Stack - to end up too close to the left edge.

By following the Golden Ratio on the bottom image, the subject has enough room to breath on both sides. This gives us a better idea of the total landscape and where the subjects fit within the environment.

This image of a backlit tree was captured just after sunrise at a beautiful spot called The Dallas Divide, in between Telluride and Ridgway, CO.

In this case, if the tree were placed on the right Rule of Thirds grid, the open space on the left would have simply been too much and the tree would have been too close to the right edge of the frame.

Even though the framing of the shot here was more intuitive than intentional, notice how the tree naturally falls on the Golden Ratio grid and provides a really nice balance in the composition.

When you use the Rule of Thirds grid in an image that has a lots of secondary and tertiary subjects, you don't have to worry quite as much about having too much open space on one side of the image.

However, the wider the image, the further away the primary subject can end up from the center of the frame, to the point that it almost feels like its being left out. This happens most severely when the format of the image is panoramic in shape. A square or 8x10 formatted image is more forgiving with this, but the more extreme the image aspect ratio, the worse the Rule of Thirds looks.

I would highly recommend putting the Golden Ratio to use in your own Photography.

I made mention earlier about a variation called the Golden Spiral. Again the theory is that our eyes naturally go to certain locations in an image and when we end up at the subject it reinforces the viewer's instincts.

In the image below of the kayaker on String Lake in Grand Teton, I did not plan on having him end up right on the end of the Spiral as that was just a happy accident. When you start thinking and better yet, seeing, with these Golden Ratios, I'm sure you will begin to find your Landscapes more pleasing.

By the way, when trying out the Golden Spiral, note that it can be rotated around the image to best suit the subject. You can cycle through all the options in Lightroom going to Tools, Crop Guide Overlay, choose the Golden Spiral and then hit Shift-O to cycle through the options.

The "Golden Spiral"

"Perfection is achieved, not when there is nothing more to add, but when there is nothing left to take away."

Antoine de Saint-Exupery

CHAPTER TEN

When is the Best Time for Me to Take Photos?

Sunrise? Sunset? The answer might surprise you

"THE GOLDEN HOURS" - WHY LIMIT YOUR PHOTOGRAPHY?

"SUNSET AT THE WATCHMAN" 7:55PM ZION NATIONAL PARK, SPRINGDALE, UT

As someone who loves the Western Landscapes of Arizona, Utah, Wyoming and Colorado along with the amazing collections of waterfalls in eastern Pennsylvania, I find that with a few exceptions, the "Golden Hours" are the worst times to photograph these places.

Now of course I have nothing against sunrise and sunset photographs, and I would add that two places I love for sunrise are Grand Teton and Monument Valley. Grand Teton because of its north-south orientation is a prime sunrise spot, though sunsets are not usually a highlight. Monument Valley, and its nearby cousin, Valley of the Gods, is best from sunrise to mid morning and again from mid afternoon to sunset.

Bryce Canyon has amazing shots all-day long - even at high noon - while Zion National Park is generally best from late morning to early afternoon because the deep canyons cause very dark shadows both early and late.

In Zion, one great spot for sunset is the view of The Watchman from the Virgin River Bridge - a sometimes spectacular shot from late afternoon to sunset - shown here at left.

So yes, sunsets can be beautiful! But ...

Whenever you read articles with "Top Ten Tips" about Landscape Photography, you invariably hear about how important it is to get up early (or stay around past sunset) to get the best, most dramatic colors.

Can the color at sunrise and sunset be wonderful? Absolutely! But there are many times and many places where the "Golden Hours" are meaningless. In fact, for many places it is the least desirable time of day to photograph there.

This recommendation can get so tiring and has so many exceptions that I'm going to nominate it to be in my ...

"Top Ten Meaningless Landscape Photography Tips"

Let's ignore the Top Ten lists and take a closer look at some photographs captured all through the day.

"JACKSON LAKE REFLECTIONS"

10AM GRAND TETON NATIONAL PARK, JACKSON, WY

Landscapes that have deep canyons such as Lower Yellowstone Falls, Dead Horse Point, most of Zion National Park, and Black Canyon of the Gunnison don't work well at sunrise or sunset. Dead Horse Point is good about an hour or so after sunrise but not very good near sunset. The others have a small window for the best shots because the sun needs to be overhead to get some light into the deepest shadows cast by the canyon walls.

For the waterfalls in eastern Pennsylvania, like Ricketts Glen (shown at right) and Dingmans Falls, you need mid-morning to mid-afternoon light to get through the dense trees in order to open up some of the deep shadows.

Now don't get me wrong, I'm not opposed to sunrise and sunsets and it is true that in some places, at some times, the color and light is stunningly beautiful. All I'm saying is that in many other places, these are exactly the wrong times of day to photograph there. It pays to do your homework about a place to find the best times, but even then, there are great photos to be had wherever you go, whenever you go there. It just might take slowing down and finding those hidden gems waiting for you to discover them.

"FOREST CASCADE" 10:25AM
RICKETTS GLEN STATE PARK, BENTON, PA

"JUNIPER SENTINEL" 8:30AM
DEAD HORSE POINT STATE PARK, MOAB, UT

This image taken at Dead Horse Point is about an hour after sunrise. You can still see the deep shadows below in the canyon, and they do provide a lot of shape and dimension with the contrast they create. Try to shoot much earlier and you just get a black canyon. Even though this image seems to break another rule - don't put your horizon in the middle - it works in this case as the twisted Juniper connects the land and sky. Always remember - they aren't really "Rules", they are just guidelines!

One of the favorite stops on our Ireland Photo Tour, Doonagore Castle sits on a hill overlooking the seaside village of Doolin. This tower was built in the mid-16th century and is currently a private residence.

This shot was taken at noon, and the light is fantastic! Even at midday, the sun isn't "exactly" overhead, and the lovely shadowing around the left side of the castle tower gives the structure such dimension in the landscape.

I have tried placing the tower in different positions in the frame, but the only ones that work are with the castle on the left. The way the hill and flowers roll from the right towards the structure and the distant village beyond counter the incredibly lush green landscape. What else makes the placement on the left work?

Take a look at the light on the tower. Notice that the shadow side is on the left, while the right side is sunlit. Because this is the brightest object in the scene, your eyes naturally go to it. The darker shadow on the left edge of the tower forms a slight visual block. This subliminally stops you and bounces your eyes to the right. You see the village of Doolin in the background and explore the surroundings.

This placement gives us a view from slightly above the entire scene and tells the story of the environment around the castle. You also get an idea of how incredibly lush and green the Irish Landscape really is.

"DOONAGORE CASTLE" 12PM DOOLIN, IRELAND

Even getting close to noon, the light on Gay Head Lighthouse makes for a wonderful subject. The nature of the structure's overhanging walkway makes it cast shadows all day long. The fence leads us to the tower, and bushes at right keep us from leaving the photo.

If we took this shot at or around sunrise or sunset, most or all of the foreground foliage would be in deep shadow. The cool greens in the image bring out the warm red and orange of the bricks in the lighthouse tower, something that would be lost at the begining and end of the day.

GAY HEAD LIGHT, 11:15AM

AQUINNAH, MARTHA'S VINEYARD, MA

This peaceful image was taken in the Hoh Rain Forest in the middle of the afternoon. The sun sparkling in the stream is the focal point of a very decorative composition.

Places with lots of tall foliage don't generally photograph well when the sun is low because of all the deep shadows cast by the tall trees and dense canopy. You need the sun higher in the sky so that it can get through the treetop openings, illuminate the subject and cast those beautiful shadows on the water and ground.

"SUNLIT GREEN", 3:30PM
OLYMPIC NATIONAL PARK, WA

"Composition is the art of arranging in a decorative manner the various elements which the painter uses to express his sentiments. In a picture every separate part will be visible and... everything which has no utility in the picture is for that reason harmful."

Henri Matisse

CHAPTER ELEVEN

Many Possible Shapes to Consider

The Aspect Ratio You Choose Will Change How Someone Views Your Photos

ASPECT RATIO & COMPOSITION
Landscape Photography's Secret Weapon

You might not think that the shape of your photograph makes much difference on how your images are viewed, but it really has a powerful effect.

The shape influences how a viewer enters and exits a photograph and affects how the elements flow within the image. Let's consider some options to see these effects.

At right we see the original shot as captured by the camera. It has some direction, but perhaps the train is too small in the frame. This would need to be a big print to work.

4:6 Original

8x10

1:1 Square

ASPECT RATIO IS AN OVERLOOKED BUT POWERFUL TOOL FOR LANDSCAPE PHOTOGRAPHY, ONE THAT CAN HAVE AN ENORMOUS IMPACT ON YOUR PHOTOS.

At the bottom left, on the opposite page, the 8x10 shape is almost square, but does still offer a bit of motion across the scene. The advantage for this shot is that 8x10" and 16x20" frames are common, so this is a compromise that can work.

To the right of the 8x10, a sqaure image can be interesting as since the train becomes a single, simple subject. Images like this look good as small prints and are nice when framed and hung together with three or four other related images.

The cropping at top right is my favorite of this bunch! This is a 16:9 shape - just like our TVs. It shows us the train strongly in the frame and includes enough of the environment so that we understand the story of the place.

At bottom right is a panoramic cropping. The shape does make it all about the train and the bridge by eliminating the sky and much of the river. This image works if you really want to focus just on the train.

8X10 ASPECT RATIO

When presented horizontally in Landscape Photography, an 8x10 often forces you to use too much foreground and/or too much sky. Otherwise, when you attempt to make the subject large enough in the frame, everything else feels cramped. I do find a vertical (or Portrait mode) 8x10 more usable for things like trees and lighthouses, and again, these are simple, single subjects.

When you look at the passing sunset storm in Monument Valley shown below, the placement of the formations was very limited and the sky becomes the strongest element. This shot works better in a wide format.

The problem with the 8x10 format is that unlike wider or taller formats, it doesn't offer much of a guide for the how the viewer should enter the image. Instead it relies more on the subject to guide the eyes. Since our digital cameras all capture images in a 3:2 aspect ratio, this would equate to an 8x12" frame. Try finding one of those! This forces us to crop the image when we wish to frame a print in a readily available size, otherwise the image would need custom framing.

1:1 SQUARE

Squares are a great format for simple subjects. Since all sides are the same size, a square frame has no direction. The viewer goes right to the subject, looks at it and leaves the picture. This is great for decorative images like the abstract series of reflections below.

Think single flowers, antique toys, fruit & vegetables, abstracts, etc. These are all things that look great in square frames - particularly when framed and grouped together in threes or fours.

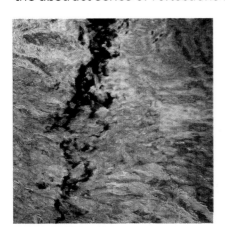 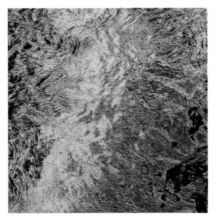 

16:9 HORIZONTAL

While a seemingly odd choice, the 16:9 shape became the standard for today's TV sets. I understand it was developed by a committee as a compromise format, but because we now see this shape everyday, it has become comfortable and actually works really well for Landscape Photography. Since this is a wider format than an 8x10, our eyes track into the photograph horizontally and most frequently from the left - like we read a book in the western world.

Because we view from left to right, our eyes follow across the landscape, hopefully leading us to the subject. By placing subtle visual barriers like a tree, rock or slight upward slope, our eyes have a tendency to move back into the image and linger a bit longer.

I personally prefer that my prints of this aspect ratio are larger - at least 24" across. 16x9 frames do exist, but I prefer having a mat around most photos. If I want to have one of these images framed, that means either custom framing, or simpler and less expensive, a custom mat to fit in a standard frame.

Top Left:	**Durango & Silverton Railroad**
Bottom Left:	**Bryce Canyon Mossy Cave Area**
Top Right:	**Red Canyon, UT**
Bottom Right:	**Dingmans Falls, PA**

16:9 VERTICALS

The 16:9 format also works very well vertically. When flipped on its side, a 16:9 looks strangely thin, but for certain subjects it works really well. I had never considered using this format, but several years ago I was speaking for Sony at a large photography trade show and they told me I would have two monitors to show images on. Both were 16:9 screens, but one of them would be hung vertically, so it was requested I prepare half of my images to accomodate the vertical monitor. Once I saw the images presented this way, I really fell in love with the appearance and shape.

Opposite its horizontal cousin, when you present someone with a vertically oriented image, you are guiding them to view the photo from the bottom up. Because of this, it is important to not present visual barriers to entering the image.

Having a physical path, a leading line or a subtle path of light at the base of the shot helps to guide the viewer into the scene. This shape of print works really well where you have narrow vertical wall spaces that would benefit form such an image. This will certainly have much more impact than sticking in a couple of 8x10s. Unfortunately, 16:9 aspect ratio frames can still be hard to find.

Durango & Silverton Railroad

Eilean Donan Castle, Scotland

Lower Yellowstone Falls

Study nature, love nature, stay close to nature. It will never fail you.

Frank Lloyd Wright

CHAPTER TWELVE

Sometimes, Bigger is Better!

An 8x10" of the Grand Canyon? Don't bother!

PANORAMAS DESERVE THEIR OWN CHAPTER!

There is no official size for a panoramic, but I am a big fan of this shape of print for my Landscape Photography. These large, super-wide images do the best job of conveying the true beauty and visual impact of a grand landscape. In fact, I'm so fond of panoramic landscapes, that maybe this should be a book of its own!

A wide image allows you not only enough room for the primary subject, but by having room on either side, you can better tell the story of the place and what the full environment adds to the subject - in essence where the subject "lives".

Because of the shape, panoramic images will usually draw you in from left to right. The viewer's eyes scan across the image to the subject and take in all of the other elements along the way. The image below is an exception because of its mirrored reflection and left and right symmetry.

Many cameras and phones today have the ability to capture super-wide panoramas. When you choose the panoramic setting, you are directed to press the shutter and then track the camera across the scene. These images can be quite fun, and are great for sharing online.

If you wish to produce large panoramic prints however, you have two choices. You can either take a shot of the entire scene and simply crop the image, or you can take a series of shots to be stitched together in software. Cropping a single shot does limit how big a print you can make, while capturing a series of shots to stitch together gives you flexibility with both focal length and size.

While this can be done with a handheld camera, for the best results, I would highly recommend using a tripod, and perhaps consider adding a panoramic tripod head. This is a subject to deal with another day, though I capture the majority of my panoramic photos with both a tripod and specialized head.

The beauty of panoramic photos is that as you gaze across the expanse, you have the opportunity to take in much more information, and this helps to further tell the story of the place.

Try to imagine a photo of the Grand Canyon as an 8x10" print - on second thought, don't bother! I have a 90" print of the Canyon in my studio (the image shown above), and it still barely does the place justice.

My favorite aspect ratios for panoramics are 2:1, 2.5:1 and 3:1. For some reason, 12" x 35" and 13.5" x 40" frames are readily available at the big craft stores.

These Super-Wide prints provide enough physical size to show all the elements that populate the environment, and last but not least, they look beautiful on the wall!

So how do we ensure that our big, beautiful panoramic compositions work visually? As with all of our photos, we want to encourage our viewers to go to the subject, and then linger and explore around the scene. Let's examine the shot above.

This scene is composed of four separate shots. There was more to the scene, but the final shot was cropped to improve the composition. Starting at the left edge, the downward slope of the mountain ridge begins our journey into the scene. We follow the ridgeline past the pines and are led up the shadowed side of the peak to the tip of Iron Mountain.

If you follow the slope down to the right, your eyes run into a taller pine tree that creates a visual block from leaving the image. These elements help to both lead you into and encourage you to stay and explore the photograph. When that happens, you begin to feel the cool air, scent of the pines and take in the beautiful contrasting colors that make up this grand vista.

"IRON MOUNTAIN" MILLION DOLLAR HIGHWAY, SILVERTON, CO

"MORMON ROW MORNING" GRAND TETON NATIONAL PARK

Grand Teton is possibly my single favorite place to photograph, and this image is one of my favorites of all the shots I have taken here. For this image to really work I will have it printed large - 60" or wider.

What this panorama accomplishes is providing a view that shows off so many of the elements, colors and mood that make this landscape so beautiful.

Try to visualize how much impact this image has at 60" across! The individual elements are large enough to draw your attention, unlike the limits of the image printed in this book.

As you come into the photo from the left, you are greeted by the trees showing their fall colors in front of the snowy mountain peaks. Continuing right, you come to the northern Moulton Barn where the fence leads to you to a solitary tree.

This tree has the visual effect of stopping your movement and you get bounced up as your eyes are drawn to the peak of Grand Teton.

Though not a strong visual block, the clouds above and alongside the peak slow you down, hopefully enough for you to re-enter the photo and explore some more. The trees on either side form those subtle visual blocks that encourage you to stay.

The Teton range is a unique landscape as there are no foothills on the east side. The eastern valley is fairly flat at around 7,000 ft. elevation until you reach the base of the mountains, which shoot straight up with Grand Teton peak at 13,770 feet.

That's just one of the reasons why this place offers such an amazing number of places for photography - it is truly a stunning landscape, everywhere you look!

I wanted to finish off this section on panoramic photos with a beautifully moody image of a lone walker at Ruby Beach, a beautiful spot on the Washington Coast in Olympic National Park.

Not all panoramics have to be of majestic mountains or grand landscapes. The breadth of this scene does such a nice job of telling the story of the place, and the atmosphere is at once calm, mysterious and tranquil. It's not a sunny day with postcard skies, and in many ways that makes this image more powerful.

You enter the image from the left and encounter the lone figure walking the beach. I captured this four-shot stitch quickly, as I wanted the figure to be in the opening between the left edge, the distant cliffs and the sea stack just ahead.

"PEACEFUL, MISTY MORNING" RUBY BEACH, OLYMPIC NATIONAL PARK

The small sea stack is the darkest element in the scene and it temporarily stops you as you scan across the photo. Continuing on, you follow the mist flowing onto the beach, and then are drawn to the pale green as it grows up the slopes to the pines at the top of the ridge.

The upward slope of the ridge initially leads you up, but your eyes then slide back down into the image and explore more details.

This image could have been cropped more off the right, but I felt that the green foliage on the slope helped to tell a more complete story of this place.

Visit www.joebradyphotography.com to watch a video on how this image was created!

129

"Don't shoot what it looks like. Shoot what it feels like."
David Alan Harvey

CHAPTER THIRTEEN

I'd Like to Have Sharp Photographs, Please!

You didn't travel across the Country for Blurry Images

APERTURE AND FOCUS DISTANCE
Keeping Everything Sharp

WHAT APERTURE DO YOU NEED FOR YOUR LANDSCAPES? IT DEPENDS!

"TIP OF THE WORLD" GIANT'S CAUSEWAY, BUSHMILLS, NORTHERN IRELAND • F22, 18MM, 1/10TH SEC.

There are lots of articles online about Aperture, ISO and Shutter speed and how they form something known as "The Exposure Triangle". For our Landscape Photography, we're going to look at aperture as a way to keep everything sharp in the frame.

In its simplest form, aperture is how big or small the lens opening is going into your camera. The higher the number, the smaller the opening. For example, on many lenses f2.8 or f4 would be wide open while f22 would be closed to its smallest opening.

"CASCADE IN GREEN"

DINGMANS FALLS, PA • F22, 45MM, 1.3 SEC.

"RACETRACK SUNSET"

DEATH VALLEY, CA • F22, 24MM, 1/13 SEC.

In general, the smaller the opening, the greatest the distance from near to far that will be in focus. Oh, if it were only that easy!

There are three other elements that affect what is in focus after you have selected the aperture - your distance to the nearest thing in the picture, the focal length of your lens and the size of your camera sensor. When you want to shoot a landscape that starts right at your feet (let's say 3-5 ft. Away) and goes miles into the distance, that's going to require the ultimate in focus from near to far. This means you will need to close down your aperture to at least f16 and possibly all the way closed to f22.

The images above were all shot at f22, the smallest aperture on my lens. While I might have been able to get away with a wider aperture, I really wanted to make sure that everything from right at my feet off to infinity was in sharp focus.

"SENTINEL OF THE FALLS" YELLOWSTONE NATIONAL PARK • F10, 400MM, 1/60 SEC.

The image above of Lower Yellowstone Falls is another one of my favorites. I was looking for a way to capture a different feeling of this iconic view. I happened to have a 400mm lens in my bag and decided to see what I could capture by getting close.

My aperture for this shot was f10, but I could have gone much lower - even at f5.6 - and still kept everything sharp. How is this possible?

I took this shot from a place named Artist's Point, and from there to the falls is about one mile as the crow flies. When you focus out at this distance, everything is going to be sharp. You can see this happen in the image at right of a sunrise at OxBow Bend in Grand Teton National Park. This is a four-shot panoramic stitch captured at 70mm and an aperture of only f4, yet everything is in sharp focus.

"SNOWY PEAKS" GRAND TETON NATIONAL PARK, JACKSON, WY • F5.6, 330MM, 1/800 SEC.

"OXBOW SUNRISE" GRAND TETON, JACKSON, WY • F4, 70MM, 1/100 SEC.

The Primary peak in the scene above is about 10 miles distant from the OxBow Bend Viewing Point, so as long as you focus on the subject at this distance, everything will be sharp because nothing is close by that needs to be in focus.

The image at top shows snow covered peaks in the Teton Range. This was taken at f5.6 with a focal lenght of 330mm, and again since the nearest thing in the frame is miles away, everything is in focus.

If you are confused about how much depth of field you have at a specific aperture and distance, there are a handful of Apps for both iOS and Android that will calculate this for you. They are handy tools that can help you get a grasp on the capabilities of different apertures.

Once you start to get the hang of picking the aperture, you won't need the apps anymore.

"PASSING STORM COLORS" MONUMENT VALLEY, AZ • F5,350MM, 1/250 SEC.

The photos on these two pages were all shot with with focal lengths between 24mm and 35mm. The apertures vary between f5 and f11.

The shot of the old gas pump at right shows in Lightroom that it was shot at 18mm, but since was captured with an APS-C sensor camera (Fujifilm X-T30) you would multiply by 1.5 to get the full frame equivalent of 27mm.

If you are walking around shooting with a basic kit lens - something in the 24-70mm range, then f11 is probably a good place to start. As a side note, I find that 80% of my shots are taken with a lens in this range. All this talk about apertures and image sharpness might sound scary, but with some experience, you quickly get a feel for this.

above

"NATURAL BRIDGE" BRYCE CANYON NATIONAL PARK • F11,
24MM* (THREE SHOT STITCH), 1/200 SEC.

Image at left

"14 CENTS A GALLON" TELLURIDE, CO • F8, 18MM*, 1/250 SEC.

27MM FULL FRAME EQUIVALENT

"The secret to creativity is knowing how to hide your sources."
Albert Einstein

CHAPTER FOURTEEN

Your Finished Photo Might Be Waiting for You in the Computer

Your Beautiful Photograph is worth the extra effort

FINE TUNING A COMPOSITION

One of the biggest technical challenges in Landscape Photography is that the tonal range of the scene often pushes the capabilities of your camera to its limits. Since your eyes can see so much more tonal range from bright to dark than your camera can, we often see very disappointing results on the camera screen after capturing one of these high tonal range shots. The image below is the original, raw file of Mt. Shuksan in Washington State before any adjustments were made.

An exploration of image processing with software is an important part of Photography, and I invite you to my website (www. joebradyphotography.com) for some editing How-To videos on this important subject.

Before you get there however, one thing I have already mentioned that is critical for Landscape Photography is to protect the highlights that need their detail maintained - in this case the clouds. The shadows can be opened up easily.

By bringing the image in Adobe Lightroom CC and adjusting Shadows and exposure the image was quickly transformed into Image 2. This is a great improvement of course, but there is too much lake and bushes before we get to the mountain.

If you examine the entire image more closely, you see that the entire mountain scene only takes up a bit more than a third at the top of the frame. The bushes at bottom and the reflection in the lake are so much larger than the mountains that they overpower the image.

Image 3 is cropped down to make the mountain more prominent. There is more balance to the image but unfortunately, the bushes and lake are still taking up too much of the frame. We could crop off more on the bottom of the scene, but that would mean cutting off the reflection of the mountains in the lake.

If it had been possible at the scene, the easiest way to fix this would have been to simply squat down lower to take the photo. This would have compressed the foreground and made the lake and reflection thinner.

Because of all the bushes in the way along the near shoreline, this wasn't possible, but is there a way to make this happen in the computer?

Turn the page to find out!

*Image 2
Simple slider adjust-
ments in Lightroom*

*Image 3
Cropping off the bottom
and right edge of the
photo*

In the final image at right, both the foreground and the sky were compressed using a great tool in Adobe Photoshop called "Content Aware Scale".

This tool allows you to compress parts of an image without causing too much distortion in the scene. When used properly (and with a little bit of constraint!) it can have a remarkable effect on the composition of your images. In this case we were able to compress the lake and foreground bushes vertically while keeping all of the leaves and reflection intact.

The sky was also compressed slightly to create better balance in the image, and once again, all of the clouds were brought a little bit closer to the horizon.

There are of course limits to how much you compress part of an image before it starts to distort, but with a little practice, it is an amazing tool for adjusting the perspective in Landscapes.

Visit - www.joebradyphotography.com for a step-by-step demonstration on how this image was created. You can find it under the "Landscape Composition and Editing" tab.

"AFTERNOON REFLECTIONS AT MT. SHUKSAN"
NORTH CASCADES NATIONAL PARK, WHATCOM COUNTY, WA

"One should really use the camera as though tomorrow you'd be stricken blind."

Dorothea Lange

CHAPTER FIFTEEN

Where Do We Go From Here With Our Photography?

Practice, Explore and Learn How to Shape Your Raw Files

WHAT ARE THE NEXT STEPS?

You've made it to the end of the book and I am honored by your interest and investment of time, so I would like to offer some next steps. Photography in general and Landscape Photography in particular are pursuits you never actually master. No matter your skill level, there is always more to learn, more to experience, more to take in, more room to grow.

Just like any other skill, photography requires practice. Once you have mastered your gear to the point that its use become automatic, it's then time to search for the elements and compositions that connect with your passions.

In essence, capture and create the images that make you smile! There is a great quote that sums up our desire to visit and photograph new places:

"If you want to take better photographs, stand in front of more interesting stuff"

Jim Richardson, National Geographic Photographer

There is some tongue-in-cheek here, because the most mundane subjects can be made interesting pieces of art with our creativity. But if Landscape, Travel and/or Wildlife photography is what excites you, consider making an investment in visiting places that have the elements which fuel those desires.

"DEEP AND DARK" BLACK CANYON OF THE GUNNISON NP

VISIT SOME NEW PLACES

I would recommend looking into joining a Photography Workshop that has a focus on your specific interests. The benefits of Workshops are many, but spending time with others who share your passion for photography can be a great way to expand your view. As a simple solution, look for a local camera club, as many of them offer outings for their groups. It's amazing how you can stand next to another photographer and get a completely different image.

My wife Diane is an accomplished photographer and since we are attracted to different elements in a scene, when you look at our photos, you sometimes wouldn't guess that were even at the same location.

When you travel with a truly experienced instructor, you will be with someone who knows the place and who also (hopefully!) knows when and where to go for the best photo opportunities. In addition to focusing on composition, one of the areas I concentrate on is really knowing the locations we explore, and I understand how and when to get the best shots in each place we visit.

There is something else remaining that must be addressed, because it is a critical component ...

"FLOATING ROCK AT THE RACETRACK" DEATH VALLEY NP

YOU NEED TO LEARN IMAGE PROCESSING!

"MOUNTAINS MAJESTY" SILVERTON, CO

I have heard some photographers say that in photography, you should "get it right in the camera".

When I shoot portraits in a studio and have complete control of lighting power and the ratios of light to dark, you can get pretty close to getting it perfect in the camera. In Landscape Photography, I'm sorry to say, that in the vast majority of cases, it simply doesn't work that way because nature doesn't cooperate.

The biggest problem is that our cameras don't see the way our eyes do. Digital cameras are much more limited in tonal range - the ability to capture from light to dark - than what our eyes can see. Since the most dramatic Landscapes often have very high ratios of light to dark, the cameras and more importantly the image processing softwares like Lightroom and Photoshop fail here - unless we take control and adjust the image.

But there's more ...

Our digital cameras only assign one color temperature to a scene, when in reality, most scenes have multiple temperatures from cool to warm light.

GET OUTSIDE AND EXPLORE

"DAWN APPROACHES" MONUMENT VALLEY TRIBAL PARK

For example, on a bright sunny day, a "daylight" color temperature setting would work pretty well. But what about places darkened by passing clouds, or deep shadows from trees and buildings?

The color in shadow is much bluer than if they had been directly illuminated by the sun. When you view the scene, your brain automatically corrects the color temperature, but your camera can't do that.

There's another reason why we need to shape our images with light and color ...

"Dodging and burning are steps to take care of mistakes God made in establishing tonal relationships."

Ansel Adams

Once again, tongue-in-cheek, but accurate at the same time. Though he worked in the darkroom, his comments still stand because image editing with programs like Photoshop and Lightroom is today's darkroom.

The purpose of this book isn't to teach image editing, but that is something I spend a lot of time doing. To provide some demonstrations that may begin to offer some help, I've added a page to my website (www.joebradyphotography.com) with some links to image editing demonstrations using both programs.

CONCLUSION

Like all creative pursuits, photography is better accomplished when your mind is clear and free from stress. It is a scientific fact that our eyes see in more of a "tunnel vision" when our body and minds are under seige or stress - think of it as a visual "fight or flight" response.

Landscape Photography can be one of the most joyful and stress reducing activities we can pursue. Even if the weather is lousy, you still had the opportunity to be outdoors.

There is a wonderful article with an audio option on NPR titled "Forest Bathing: A Retreat to Nature Can Boost Immunity and Mood"*. Now of course, there is no actual "bathing" happening, but rather taking the time to surround yourself with nature and soak in all of the place with all of your senses.

Since you are interested enough in Landscape Photography to read this book, you already have a love of nature and the way it makes you feel. Be mindful of what you are feeling when you have the good fortune to visit a beautiful place. When you get away from the "tunnel vision" caused by stress, you learn to see everything around, both near and far.

That is the first step towards improving your Landscape Photography, and I truly wish for you the joy and satisfaction that brings.

My Best Regards,
Joe Brady

"Which of my photographs is my favorite?
The one I'm going to take tomorrow."
Imogen Cunningham

* https://n.pr/3ytsyb5

Made in the USA
Columbia, SC
29 March 2022

58243293R00084